Read | Trace | Write

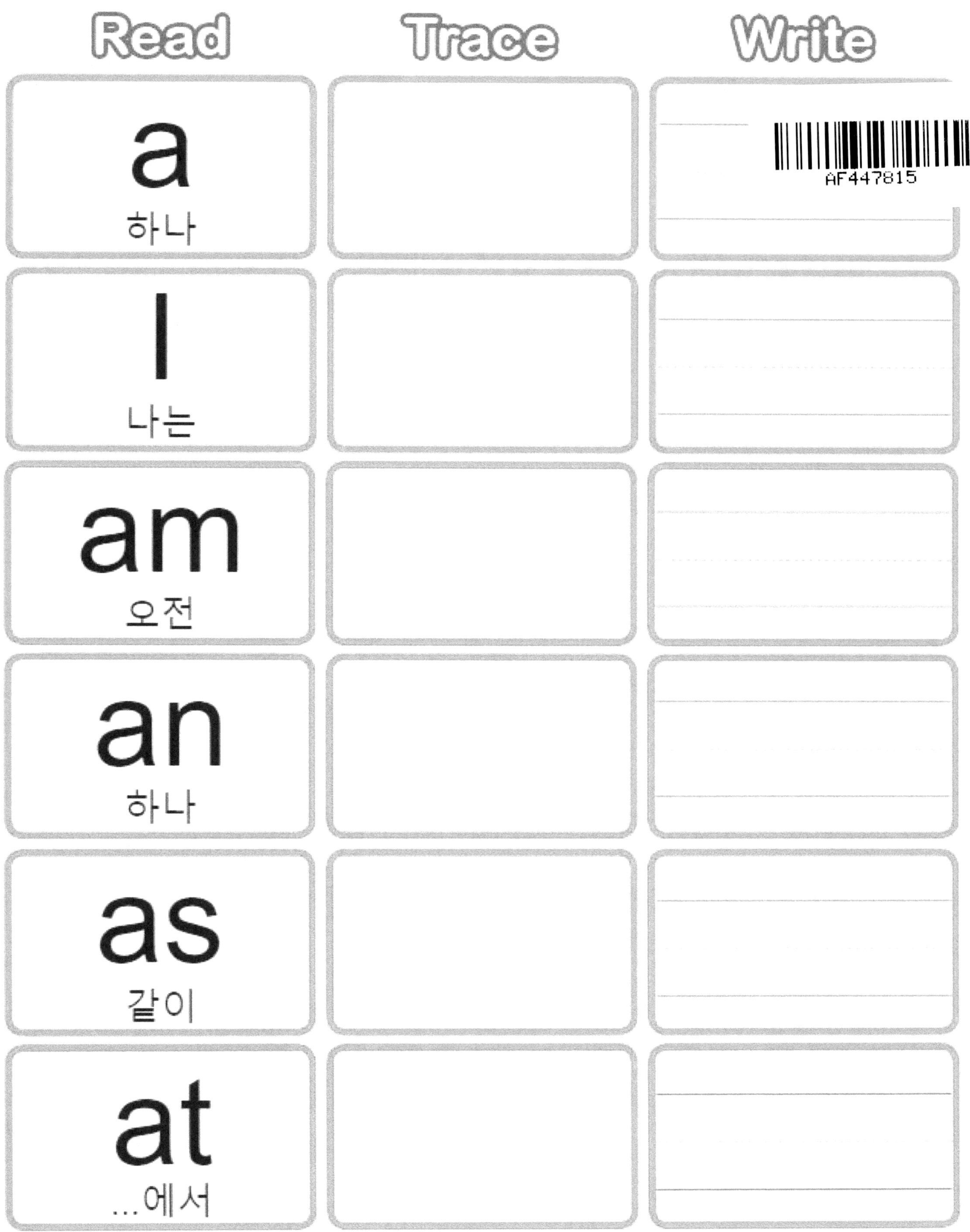

Read and write the sentence!

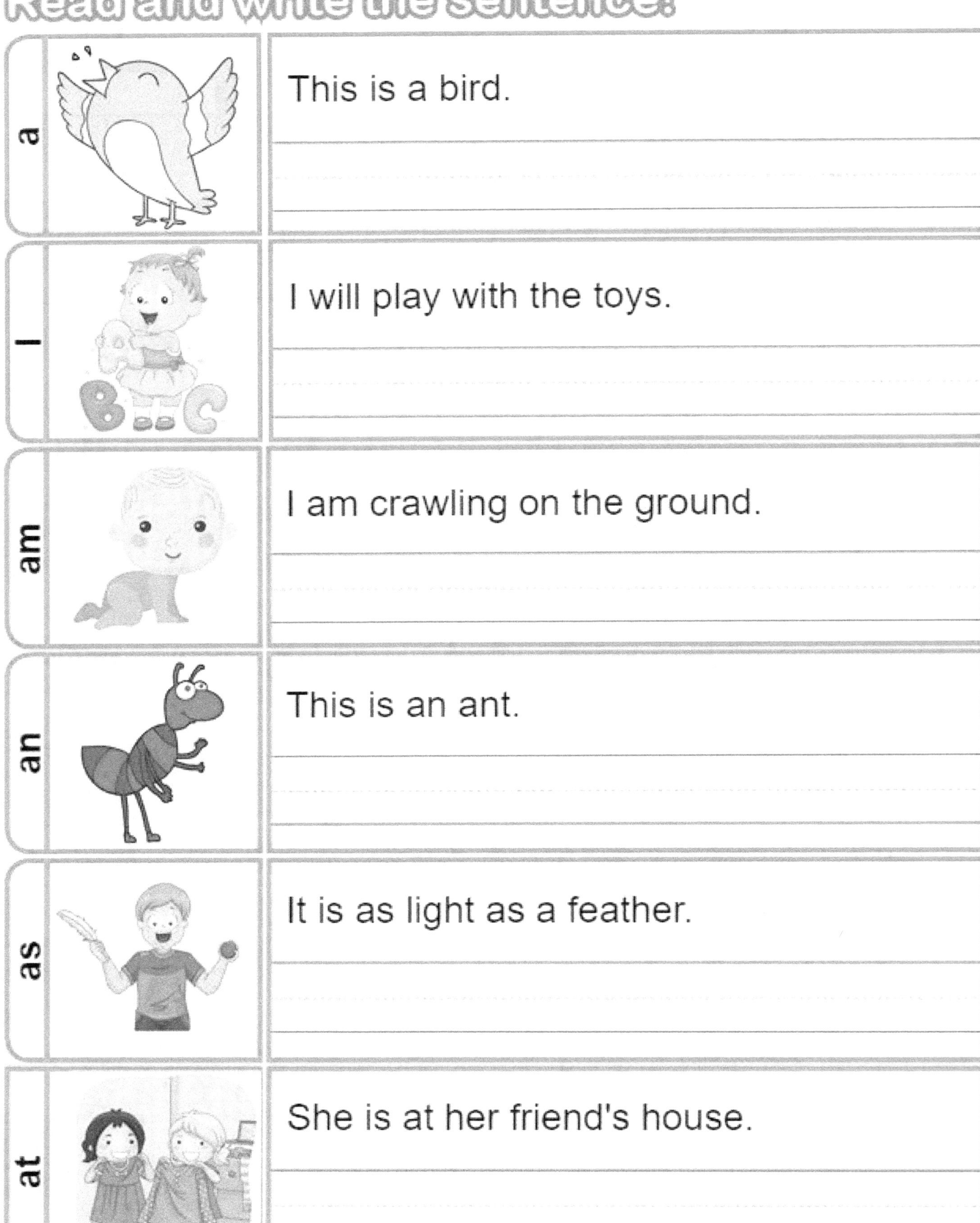

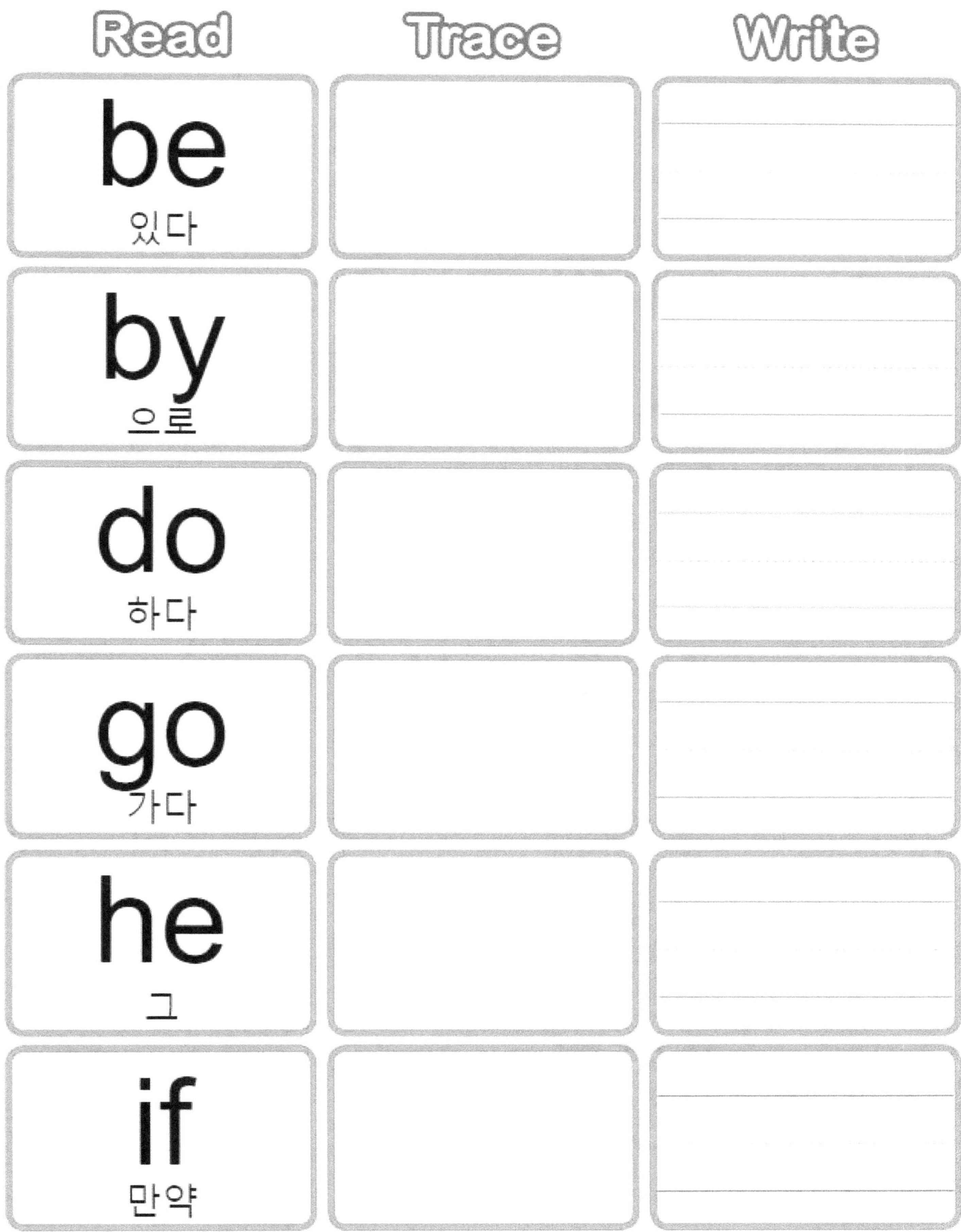
Read
Trace
Write
be
있다
by
으로
do
하다
go
가다
he
그
if
만약

Read and write the sentence!

Read
Trace
Write
in
에
is
이다
it
그것
me
나를
my
나의
no
아니

Read and write the sentence!

in		The baby is in the bath.
is		The cat is happy.
it		It is my toy.
me		It's me.
my		This is my nose.
no		No, I will not!

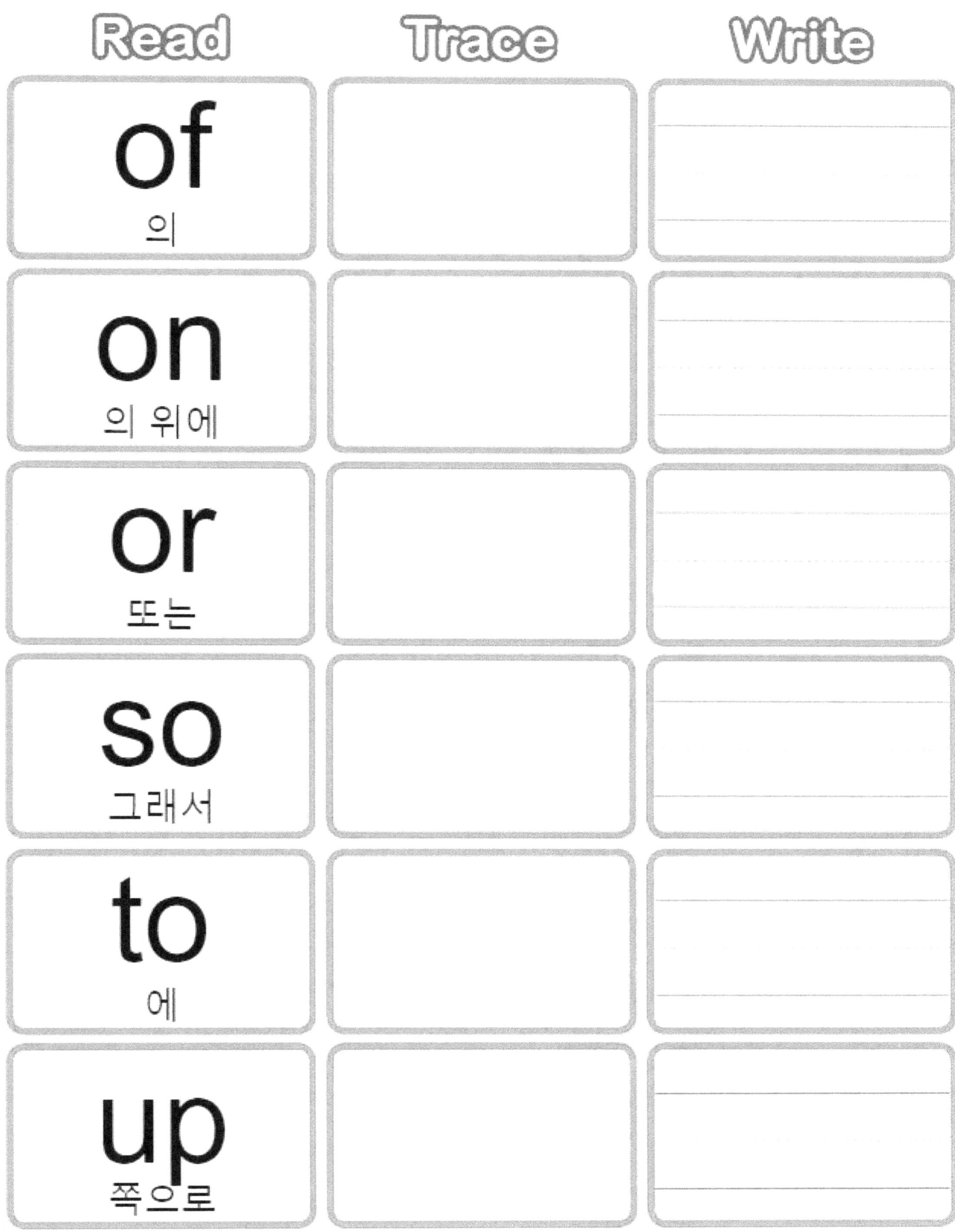

Read
Trace
Write
of
의
on
의 위에
or
또는
so
그래서
to
에
up
쪽으로

Read and write the sentence!

of	One of the boys is my son.
on	He turns on the light.
or	Should I eat this or that?
so	This is so yummy.
to	She will read to the end.
up	He is stacking the colorful blocks.

Read	Trace	Write
us 우리		
we 우리		
all 모두		
and 과		
any 어떤		
are 아르		

Read and write the sentence!

us	Both of us are walking.
we	We are helping to make a house.
all	We are all dancing together.
and	My brother and I are playing.
any	They can read any books.
are	The eggs are colorful.

Read
Trace
Write
ask
물어보기
ate
먹었다
bed
침대
big
큰
box
상자
boy
소년

Read and write the sentence!

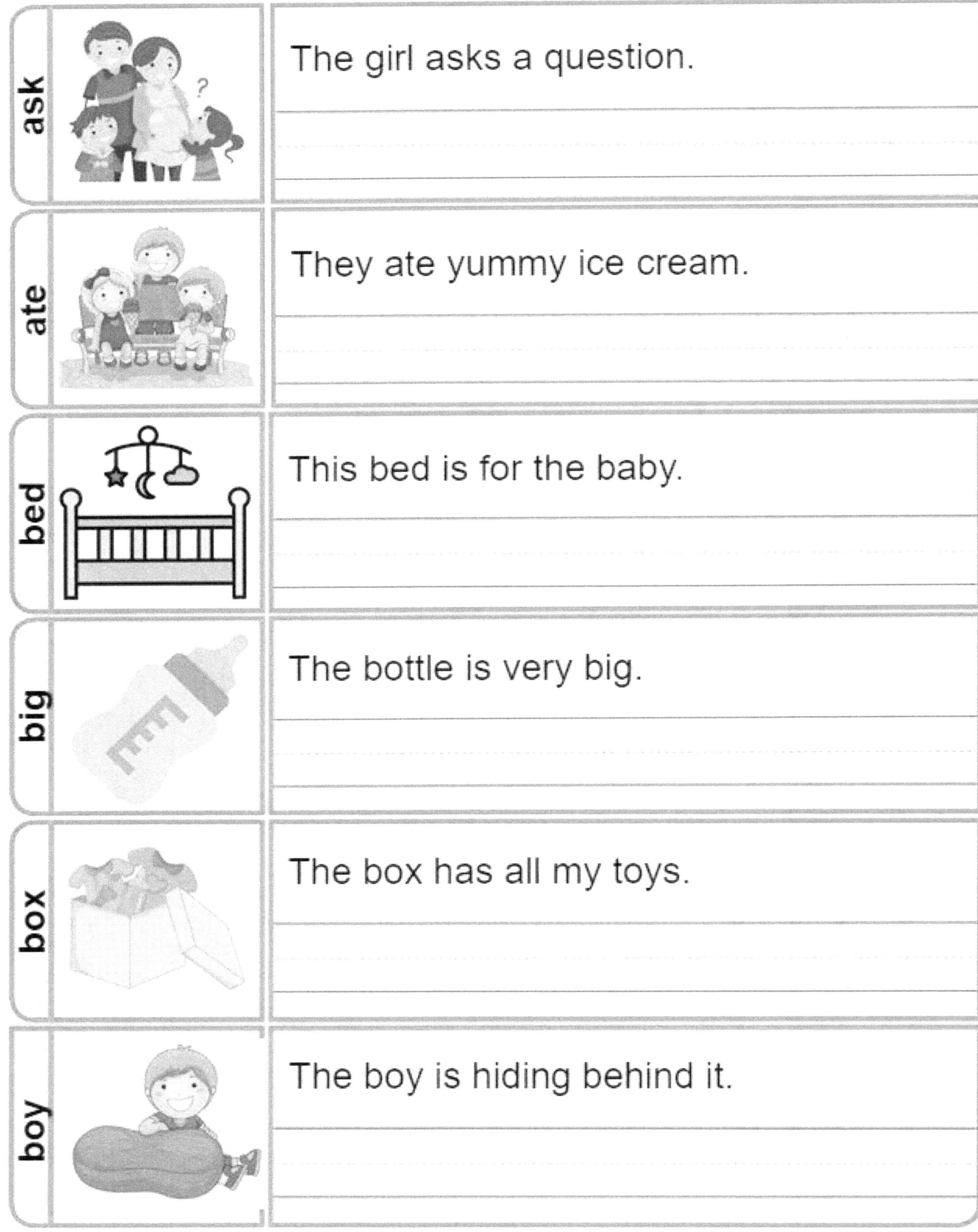

ask	The girl asks a question.
ate	They ate yummy ice cream.
bed	This bed is for the baby.
big	The bottle is very big.
box	The box has all my toys.
boy	The boy is hiding behind it.

Read
Trace
Write
but
그러나
buy
구입
can
할 수 있다
car
차
cat
고양이
cow
소

but — I want to go, but my son doesn't.

buy — He buys lots of stuff.

can — The baby will drink milk from the can.

car — The car is red.

cat — The cat is sad.

cow — The cow is funny.

Read
Trace
Write
cut
절단
day
일
did
했어
dog
개
eat
먹다
egg
계란

Read and write the sentence!

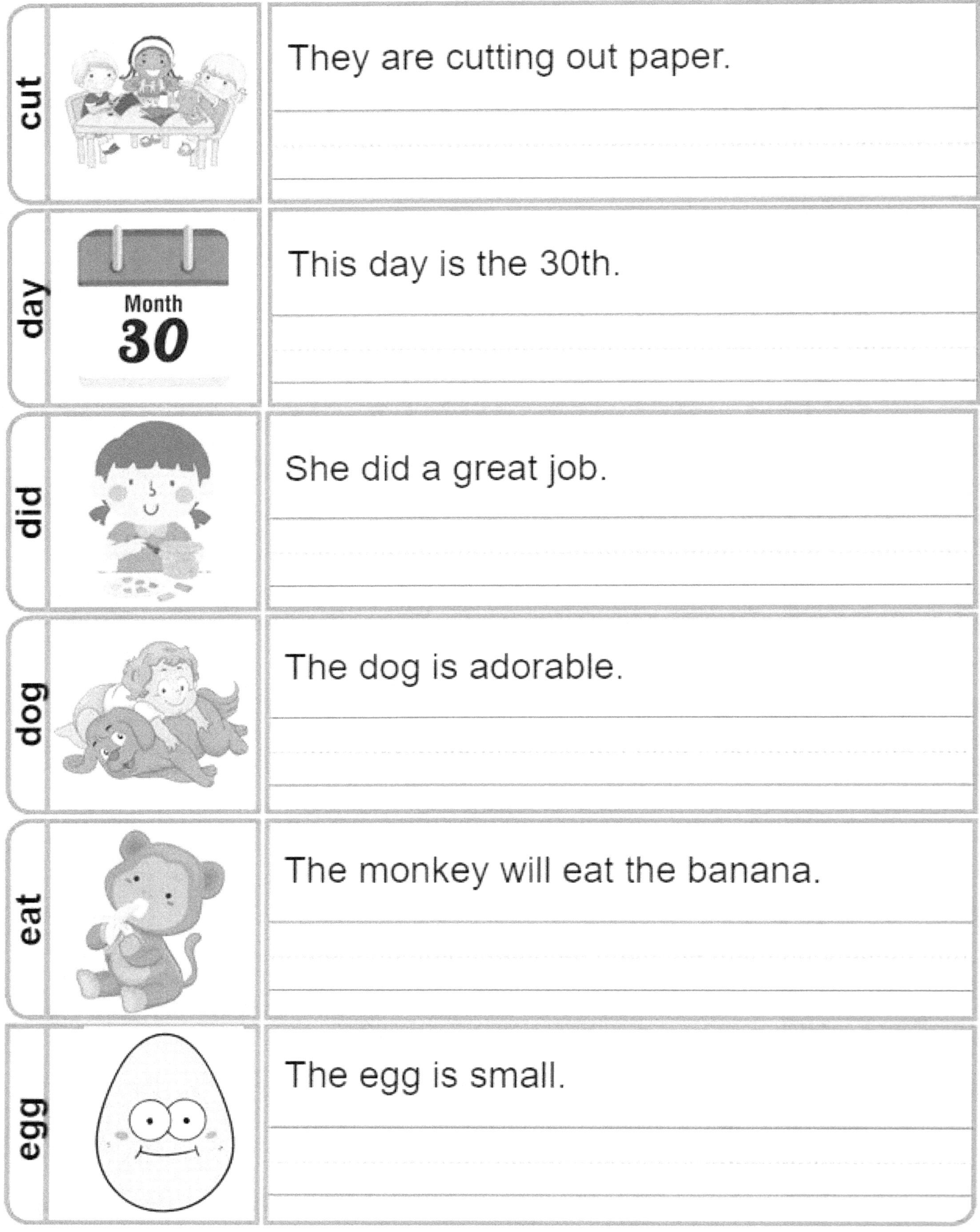

cut	They are cutting out paper.
day	This day is the 30th.
did	She did a great job.
dog	The dog is adorable.
eat	The monkey will eat the banana.
egg	The egg is small.

Read
Trace
Write
eye
눈
far
멀리
fly
파리
for
에 대한
get
가져 오기
got
있어

Read and write the sentence!

Read
Trace
Write
had
했다
has
있다
her
그녀
him
그를
his
그의
hot
뜨거운

had		He had a big tummy.
has		She has a doll.
her		She has her trolley.
him		I gave my hat to him.
his		His cheeks are big.
hot		It is hot on the beach.

Read
Trace
Write
how
어떻게
its
이것의
leg
다리
let
허락하다
man
남자
may
할 수있다

how		How many blocks are there?
its		Its legs are short.
leg		His legs are short.
let		Let me come in!
man		The man is a vet.
may		May I have more?

Read	Trace	Write

men
남자들

new
새로운

not
아니

now
지금

off
떨어져서

old
낡은

Read and write the sentence!

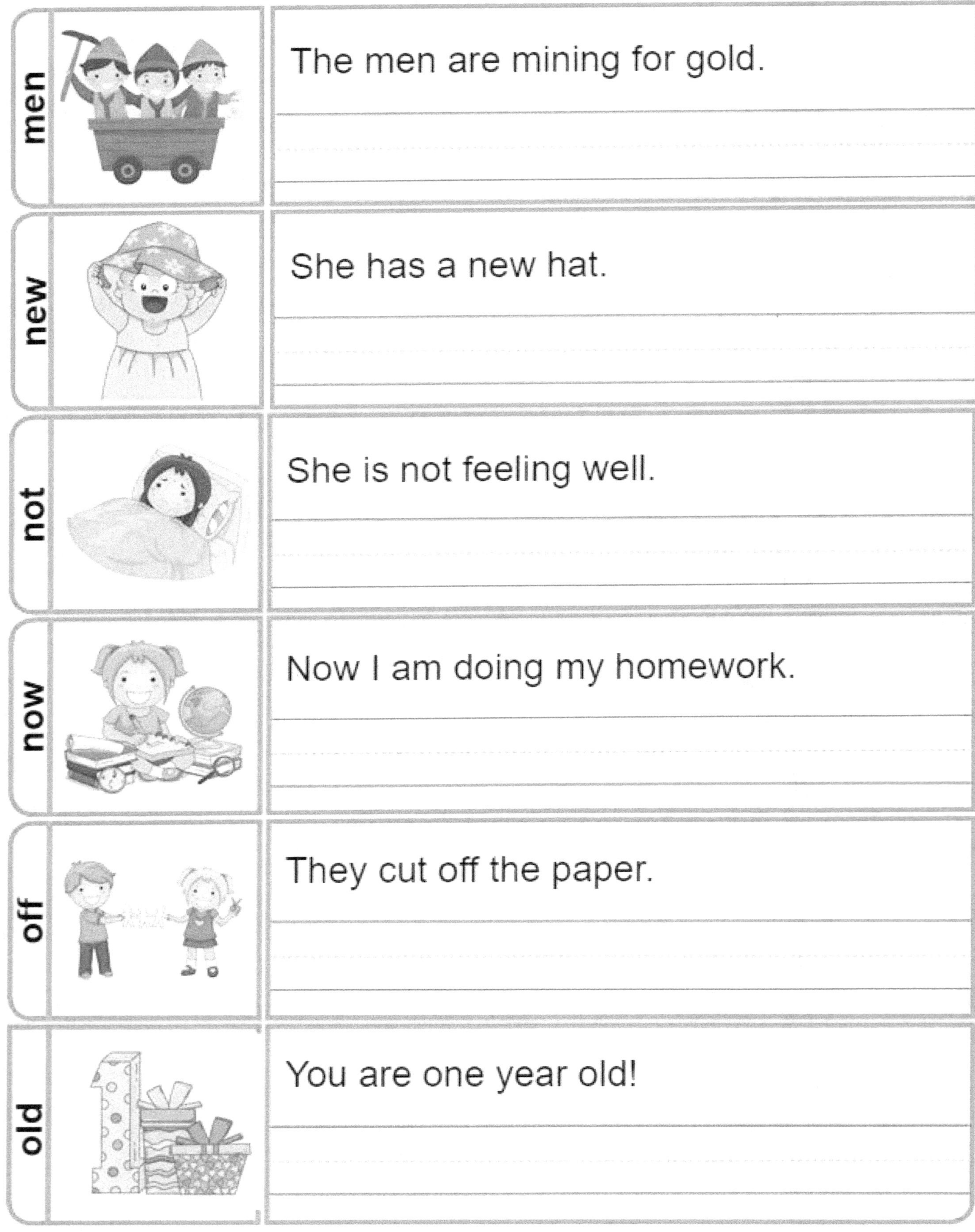

Read
Trace
Write
one
하나
our
우리의
out
밖
own
개인적인
pig
돼지
put
놓다

Read and write the sentence!

one		The panda says one.
our		This is our room.
out		He will go out.
own		The man owns a computer.
pig		She is sleeping on her pig.
put		She is putting an arm around her daughter.

Read	Trace	Write

Read and write the sentence!

Word	Picture	Sentence
ran		She ran back home.
red		The bus is red.
run		He is running away from the bats.
saw		He saw something.
say		You should always say Please.
see		They see something in the sky.

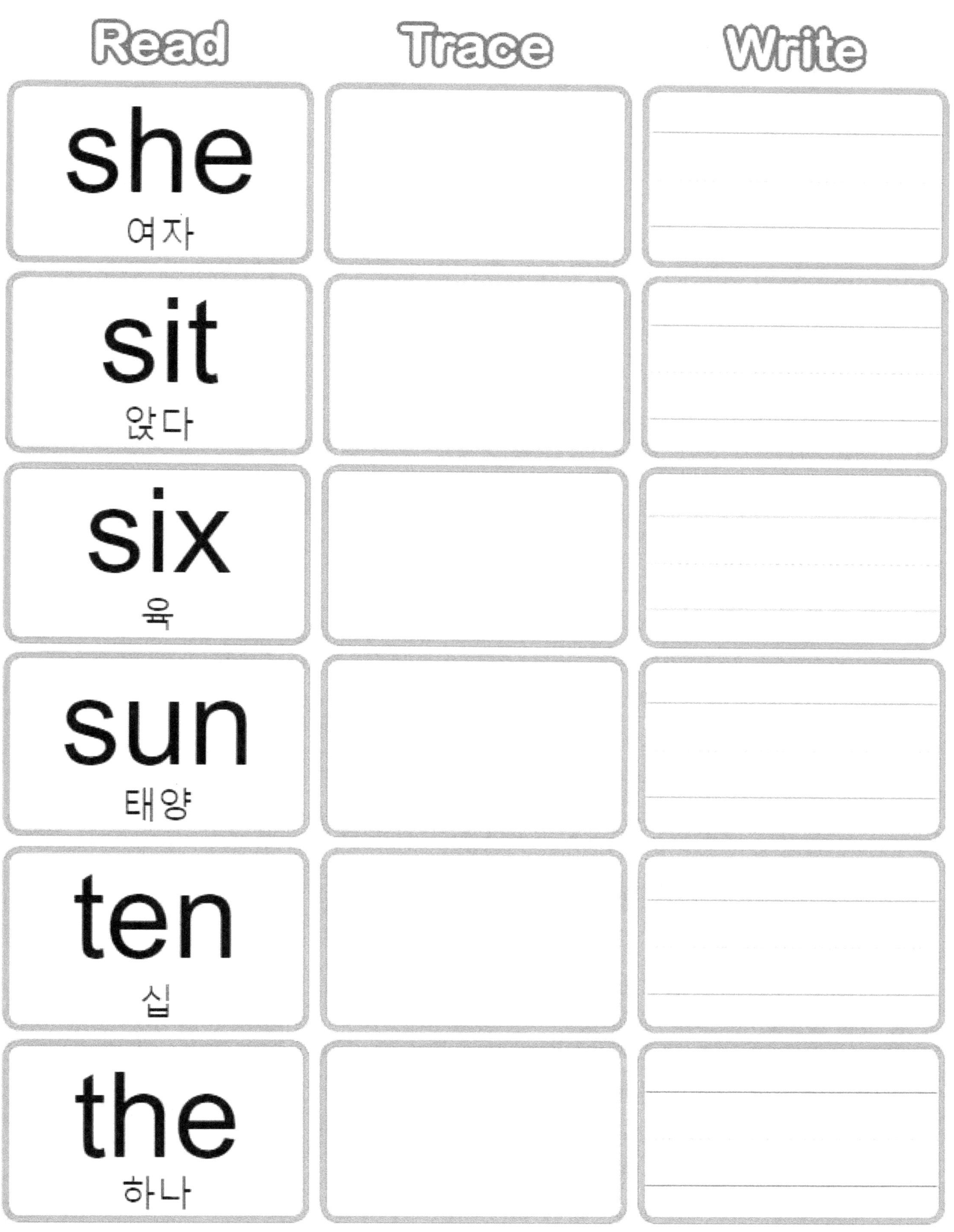
Read
Trace
Write
she
여자
sit
앉다
six
육
sun
태양
ten
십
the
하나

Read and write the sentence!

Read	Trace	Write
too 너무		
top 상단		
toy 장난감		
try 시험		
two 두		
use 사용하다		

Read and write the sentence!

too	The bear is too cute.
top	The pot is on the top.
toy	The baby has lots of toys.
try	We try to be kind to him.
two	Today you have turned two.
use	I use my toothpaste and toothbrush.

Read
Trace
Write
was
였다
way
방법
who
뭐
why
왜
yes
예
you
당신

Read and write the sentence!

Read	Trace	Write
away 떨어져		
baby 아가		
back 뒤		
ball 공		
bear 곰		
been 였다		

Read and write the sentence!

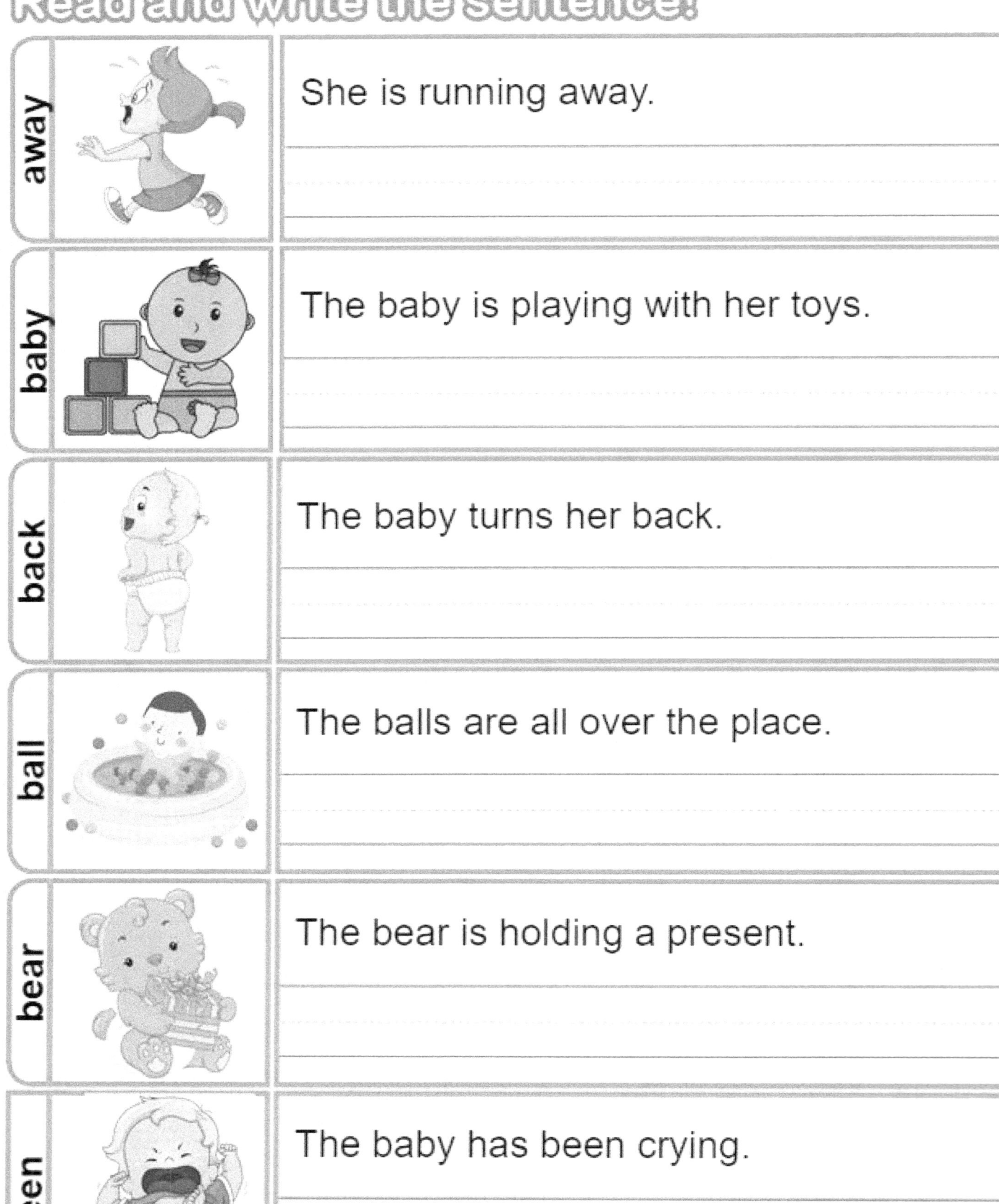

Read
Trace
Write
bell
벨
best
베스트
bird
새
blue
푸른
boat
보트
both
양자 모두

Read and write the sentence!

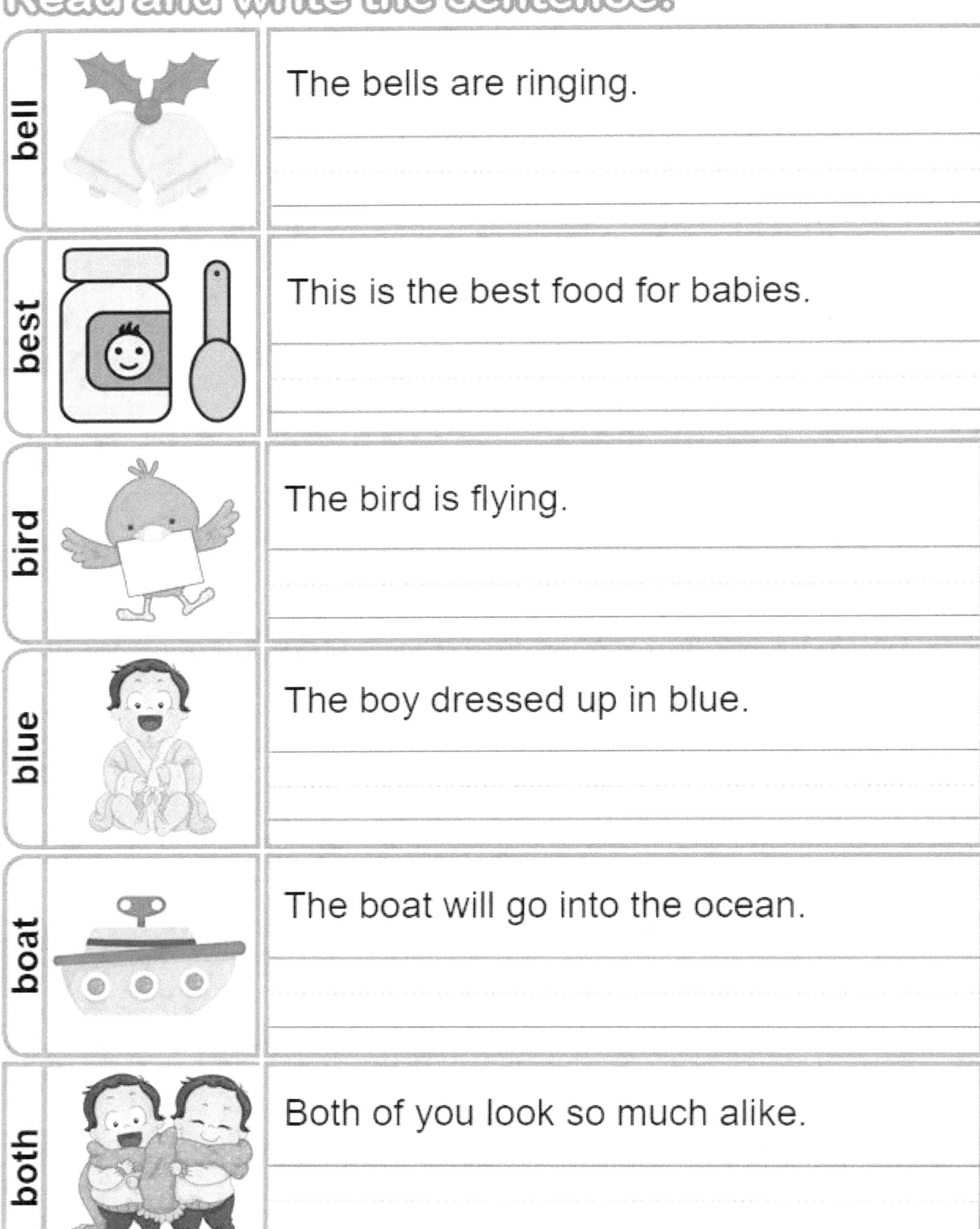

bell	The bells are ringing.
best	This is the best food for babies.
bird	The bird is flying.
blue	The boy dressed up in blue.
boat	The boat will go into the ocean.
both	Both of you look so much alike.

Read | Trace | Write

Read	Trace	Write
cake 케이크		
call 요구		
came 왔다		
coat 코트		
cold 춥다		
come 왔다		

Read and write the sentence!

cake	The cake is for your birthday.
call	She is calling for somebody.
came	She came with her bag.
coat	The girl is wearing her coat.
cold	The baby feels cold.
come	Come here to the slide!

Read	Trace	Write
corn 옥수수		
does 않습니다		
doll 인형		
done 끝난		
door 문		
down 내려가는		

corn		The corn tastes good.
does		Does that thing taste bad?
doll		She is hugging her doll.
done		I've done reading my book.
door		They open the door.
down		The boy turns his head down.

Read	Trace	Write
draw 무승부		
duck 오리		
fall 가을		
farm 농장		
fast 빠른		
feet 발		

Read and write the sentence!

draw	They all draw pictures.
duck	The duck is yellow.
fall	He fell down from the swing.
farm	He grows crops at his farm.
fast	She is doing everything very fast.
feet	I touch my feet.

Read
Trace
Write

find
찾기

fire
불

fish
물고기

five
다섯

four
네

from
...에서

Read and write the sentence!

find	They are finding something.
fire	The fire is blazing and dangerous.
fish	The fish are swimming in the ocean.
five	You get birthday gifts for turning five.
four	The lion is turning four today.
from	She will draw a picture of her flower.

Read	Trace	Write
full 완전한		
game 계략		
gave 준		
girl 소녀		
give 주기		
goes 간다		

Read and write the sentence!

full	His backpack is full of things.
game	This game is enjoyable.
gave	She gave something to her friend.
girl	The girl is sad because of something.
give	The baby gives her mommy something.
goes	She goes to the forest.

Read
Trace
Write
good
좋은
grow
자라다
hand
손
have
있다
head
머리
help
도움

Read and write the sentence!

good		The baby is acting very well today.
grow		My plant will grow!
hand		My hand is touching the wall.
have		She will have lots of friends.
head		My head is round.
help		They help each other wash the clothes.

Read
Trace
Write

here
여기

hill
언덕

hold
보류

home
집

hurt
상처

into
으로

Read and write the sentence!

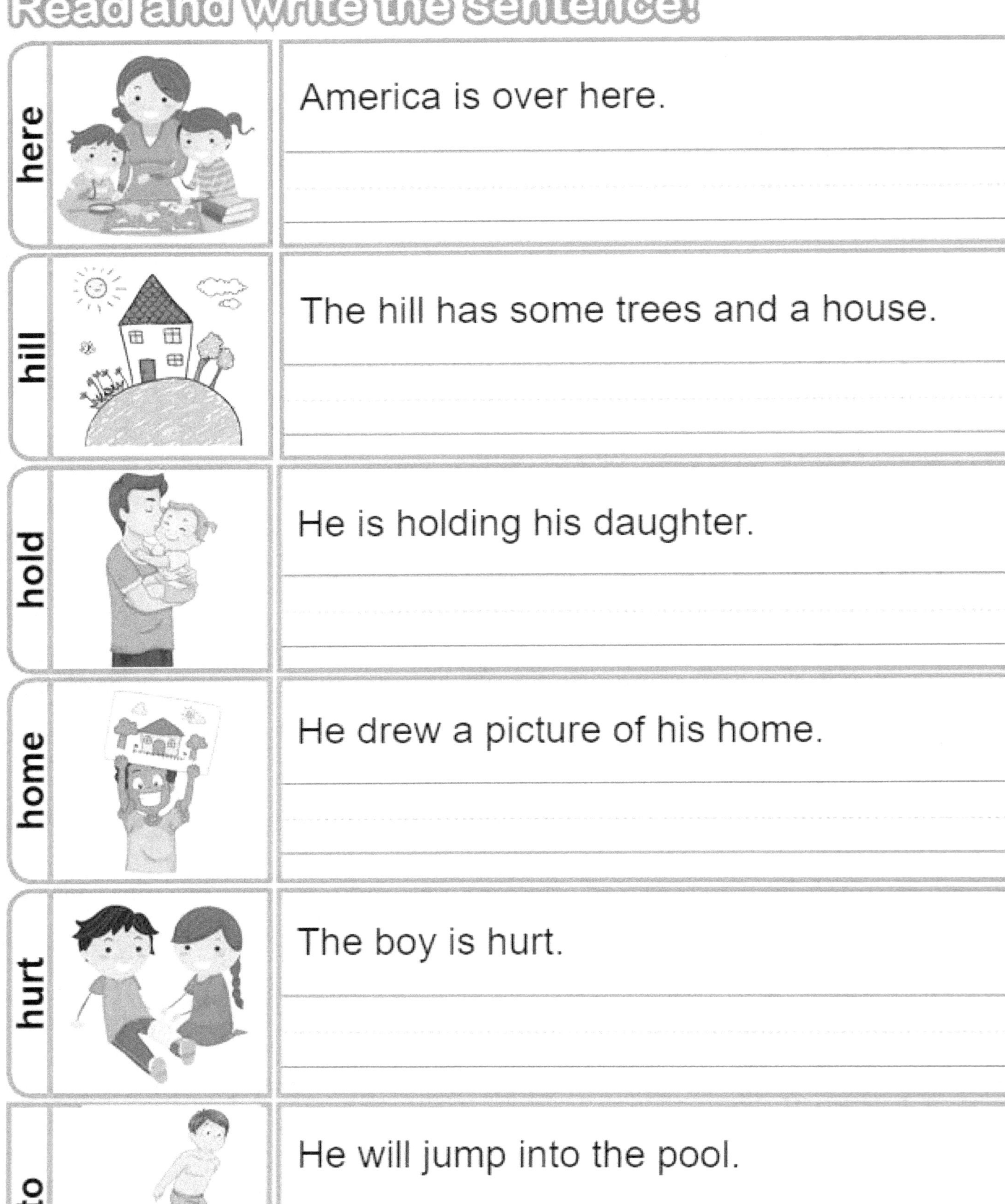

here	America is over here.
hill	The hill has some trees and a house.
hold	He is holding his daughter.
home	He drew a picture of his home.
hurt	The boy is hurt.
into	He will jump into the pool.

Read
Trace
Write

jump
도약

just
다만

keep
유지

kind
종류

know
알고있다

like
처럼

Read and write the sentence!

jump		The cat jumped on the cushion.
just		The arrival of the plane just arrived.
keep		She keeps thinking about it.
kind		The woman is kind to the girl.
know		They know that they will go over there.
like		He likes to ride on the horse.

Read
Trace
Write
live
라이브
long
긴
look
보기
made
만든
make
만든
many
많은

Read and write the sentence!

live		They all live together.
long		The pencil is very long.
look		They are looking at something.
made		They made a promise.
make		They are going to make something.
many		He has many shirts.

Read
Trace
Write
milk
우유
much
많은
must
필요한 것
name
이름
nest
둥지
once
한번

Read and write the sentence!

milk	I have milk for breakfast.
much	I like to eat this very much.
must	I must do all my homework.
name	My name is Joe.
nest	The bird has a nest.
once	He once liked to look at his computer.

Read	Trace	Write
only 뿐		
open 열다		
over 위에		
pick 선택		
play 플레이		
pull 손잡이		

Read and write the sentence!

There is only one student.

He wants to open the door.

The class is over.

She picked up something.

They like to play together.

She is pulling on her friend's hair.

Read
Trace
Write
rain
비
read
읽다
ride
타기
ring
반지
said
말했다
seed
씨

Read and write the sentence!

rain		The rain is not going to hit us.
read		She likes to read books.
ride		The baby is riding on a toy horse.
ring		The bird is holding a ring in its beak.
said		She said hello to her neighbor.
seed		The seeds are going to plant.

Read	Trace	Write

shoe
구두

show
보여 주다

sing
노래

snow
눈

some
약간

song
노래

Read and write the sentence!

shoe		Her shoes are cute and purple.
show		This map shows the location.
sing		The baby can sing along.
snow		I like to play snow.
some		These are some of my toys.
song		I will sing a song in the talent show.

Read	Trace	Write
soon 곧		
stop 중지		
take 갖다		
tell 텔		
that 그		
them 그들		

Read and write the sentence!

soon		The eggs will hatch soon.
stop		The teacher says to stop.
take		They take some flowers.
tell		She is telling a story.
that		That bird dressed up as Santa.
them		He likes to eat them.

Read
Trace
Write
then
그때
they
그들
this
이
time
시각
tree
나무
upon
...에

Read and write the sentence!

word	picture	sentence
then		Then, I will go to bed.
they		They are running to school.
this		This is my duck.
time		The time always moves on.
tree		There are lots of green trees in the park.
upon		Once upon a time, there was a princess.

Read	Trace	Write
very 대단히		
walk 산책		
want 필요		
warm 따뜻한		
wash 빨래		
well 잘		

very	The baby is lovely.
walk	They are walking on the sidewalk.
want	The baby wants more milk.
warm	The bath is warm.
wash	She is going to wash the dishes.
well	He can save money well.

Read	Trace	Write
went 갔다		
were 아르		
what 뭐		
when 언제		
will 의지		
wind 바람		

Read and write the sentence!

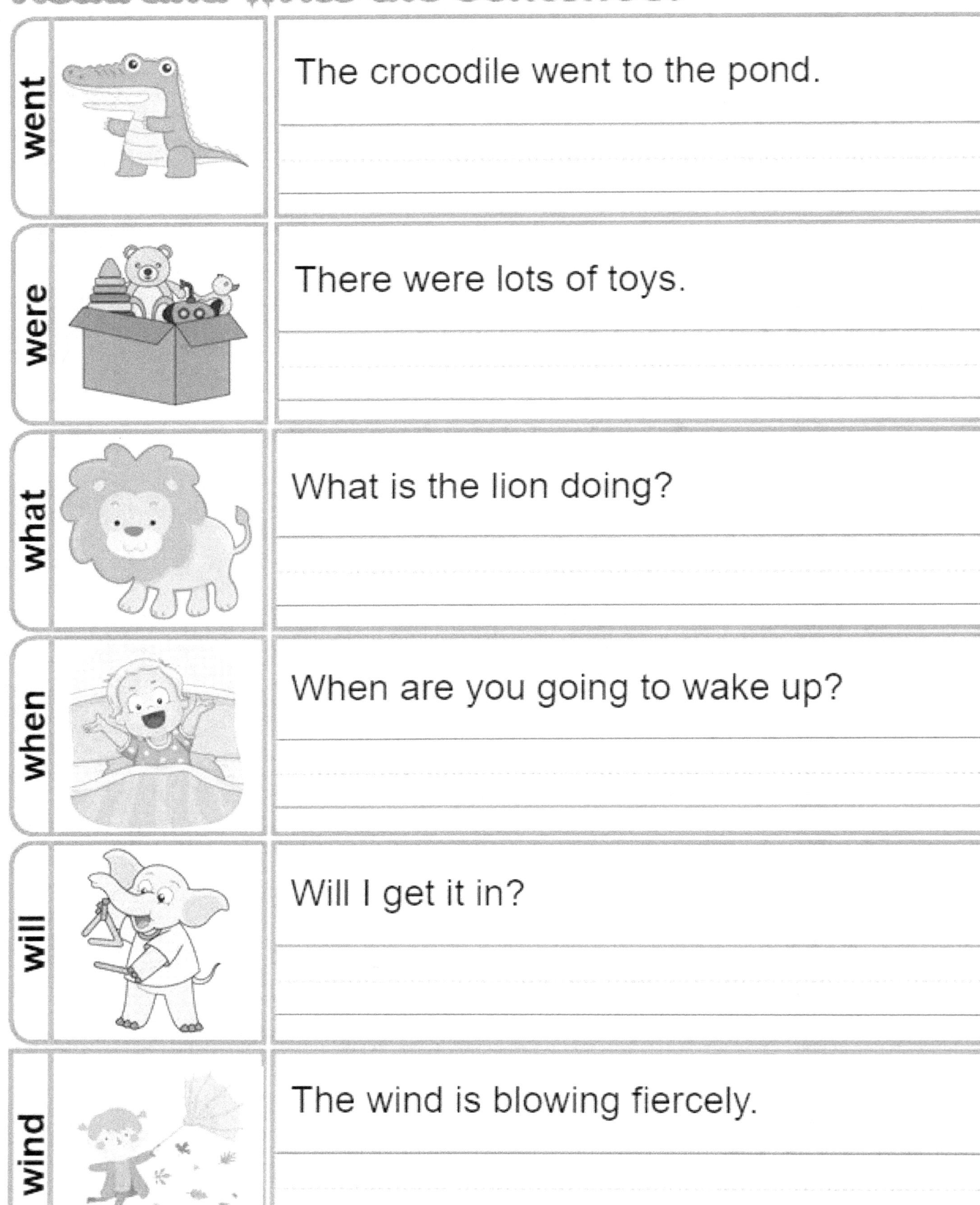

Read
Trace
Write
wish
소원
with
와
wood
나무
work
작업
your
너의
about
약

wish		I wish you a happy Christmas!
with		He is with his sister.
wood		He is stacking up wooden blocks.
work		He is going to work in his tractor.
your		Your baby is wearing a yellow suit.
about		It's about to be 12:30.

Read
Trace
Write
after
후
again
다시
apple
사과
black
검은
bread
빵
bring
가져오다

Read and write the sentence!

after		The teacher calmed them after they fought.
again		He did it again!
apple		The apple is red and juicy.
black		The crow is black.
bread		My breakfast is bread and jam.
bring		He is bringing his project.

Read	Trace	Write
brown 갈색		
carry 나르다		
chair 의자		
clean 깨끗한		
could 할 수있다		
don't 하지마		

Read and write the sentence!

brown		Her stuffed animal is a brown bear.
carry		He is carrying a big crayon.
chair		He is sitting on his chair.
clean		He needs to clean up.
could		The baby could do push-ups.
don't		Don't do that!

<table>
<tr><th>Read</th><th>Trace</th><th>Write</th></tr>
<tr><td>drink
음주</td><td></td><td></td></tr>
<tr><td>eight
여덟</td><td></td><td></td></tr>
<tr><td>every
...마다</td><td></td><td></td></tr>
<tr><td>first
먼저</td><td></td><td></td></tr>
<tr><td>floor
바닥</td><td></td><td></td></tr>
<tr><td>found
녹이다</td><td></td><td></td></tr>
</table>

Read and write the sentence!

drink	The baby likes to drink water.
eight	You get eight gifts for turning eight!
every	Every book is colorful.
first	We won first place.
floor	She is sitting on the floor.
found	It found a hat in the streets.

Read
Trace
Write
funny
이상한
going
가다
grass
잔디
green
초록
horse
말
house
집

Read and write the sentence!

funny	The rabbit thinks the joke is funny.
going	The bear is going to eat all the honey.
grass	The goat eats grass on the hill.
green	The turtle that is walking is green.
horse	The horse is magical.
house	They lived in that house.

Read
Trace
Write
kitty
고양이
laugh
웃음
light
빛
money
돈
never
못
night
밤

Read and write the sentence!

kitty	The kitties are charming.
laugh	They are laughing while playing.
light	The boy will turn on the lights.
money	I have earned a lot of money.
never	The bear never ate ice cream before.
night	I will sleep on my blanket at night.

<table>
<tr><th>Read</th><th>Trace</th><th>Write</th></tr>
<tr><td>paper
종이</td><td></td><td></td></tr>
<tr><td>party
파티</td><td></td><td></td></tr>
<tr><td>right
옳은</td><td></td><td></td></tr>
<tr><td>round
일주</td><td></td><td></td></tr>
<tr><td>seven
일곱</td><td></td><td></td></tr>
<tr><td>shall
할까요</td><td></td><td></td></tr>
</table>

Read and write the sentence!

paper	I will draw on the paper for a project.
party	The party will be for her birthday.
right	They say we have to go right.
round	The frogs' eyes are round.
seven	The monkey can count to seven.
shall	Shall I make a garden?

Read
Trace
Write
sheep
양
sleep
자다
small
작은
start
스타트
stick
스틱
table
표

Read and write the sentence!

sheep		The sheep have a bell around its neck.
sleep		I will go to sleep in my comfortable bed.
small		The small baby will crawl to its crib.
start		She will start sleeping soon.
stick		He has some sticks to play.
table		The table has a toy on it.

Read
Trace
Write
thank
감사
their
그들의
there
그곳에
these
이들
thing
의회
think
생각한다

Read and write the sentence!

thank		He made a Thank you card for you.
their		They will enjoy their picnic.
there		There is something in front of you.
these		These are my eating material.
thing		The thing is broken.
think		She thinks about what she is going to draw.

Read	Trace	Write
those 그		
three 세		
today 오늘		
under 아래에		
watch 손목 시계		
water 물		

Read and write the sentence!

those		Those are mine.
three		She will turn three today.
today		Today is a beautiful day.
under		The puppy sleeps under the blanket.
watch		They both watch the video.
water		He is drinking water after a long soccer game.

Read
Trace
Write
where
어디
which
어느
white
하얀
would
할 것이다
write
쓰다
always
항상

Read and write the sentence!

where		Where are we?
which		The clothes which are my sisters are colorful.
white		The sheep have white wool.
would		He would tell them a story.
write		I like to write lots of stories.
always		I am always happy that it is Christmas.

<table>
<tr><th>Read</th><th>Trace</th><th>Write</th></tr>
<tr><td>around
주위에</td><td></td><td></td></tr>
<tr><td>before
전에</td><td></td><td></td></tr>
<tr><td>better
...보다 나은</td><td></td><td></td></tr>
<tr><td>farmer
농장주</td><td></td><td></td></tr>
<tr><td>father
아버지</td><td></td><td></td></tr>
<tr><td>flower
꽃</td><td></td><td></td></tr>
</table>

around	I will shuffle the shapes around.
before	Before I go to school, I kiss my mom.
better	I can make it better.
farmer	The farmer takes care of the animals.
father	My father is wearing a blue shirt.
flower	She will play with the flowers.

Read	Trace	Write
garden 정원		
ground 바닥		
letter 편지		
little 작은		
mother 어머니		
myself 자기		

Read and write the sentence!

garden		Her garden is vast and healthy.
ground		I am playing with my dog on the ground.
letter		These are the letters A, B, and C.
little		The world is small.
mother		My mother is very nice.
myself	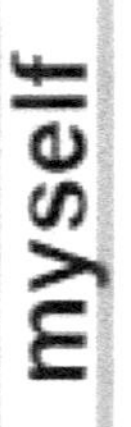	I made these by myself.

Read	Trace	Write
please 부디		
pretty 예쁜		
rabbit 토끼		
school 학교		
sister 여자 형제		
street 거리		

Read and write the sentence!

please

Please stop pulling my hair.

pretty

She made the cake very pretty.

rabbit

The rabbit is white and soft.

school

This is the school.

sister

My sister is wearing a pink dress.

street

They are walking across the street.

Read	Trace	Write
window 창문		
yellow 노랑		
because 때문에		
brother 동료		
chicken 치킨		
goodbye 안녕		

Read and write the sentence!

window

The window is open.

yellow

The ducky is yellow.

because

She will sleep because it is night.

brother

His brother is playing with him.

chicken

The chicken has hatched out of the egg.

goodbye

The animal is saying goodbye.

Read	Trace	Write
morning 아침		
picture 그림		
birthday 생신		
children 어린이		
squirrel 청설모		
together 함께		

Read and write the sentence!

morning	He likes to ride his bike in the morning.
picture	He will take a picture.
birthday	Today is my birthday!
children	The children are doing something.
squirrel	The squirrel is cute.
together	They are sharing a bed together.

www.ingramcontent.com/pod-product-compliance
Lightning Source LLC
Chambersburg PA
CBHW080839160726
47999CB00009B/2949